I dedicate this book with the utmost

gratitude to:

∞ God
~ who always has my back

∞ Edward Bozeman, Sr.
~ for allowing me to heal

∞ My Family
~ for making life interesting

∞ Mr. Coggins
~ for accepting the "Perfect Job"

FOREWORD

Several months before I returned to the United States in September 1966, Southern California Kaiser Permanent Founding Medical Director, Dr. Raymond KAY and his senior management team decided to implement the "Watts Project".

The "Project," funded by the organization's community benefit budget, would be a non-profit community service activity designed to assist Watts children and parents to deal with the problems they faced in their lives. I was hired in November 1966 to conceptualize, design, and implement "The Watts Project."

Prior to that time, I was living in London while

working and studying at the famed Tavistock Psychiatric clinic as an Advanced Casework Fellow and Fulbright scholar. The fact that I was born and raised in Harlem, and that I had ten years' experience working as a psychiatric social work therapist in a variety of communities, probably contributed to my being hired. "The Watts Project" was in its start-up stage when I first met Annette. She was eight years old. I developed an ongoing relationship with Annette's family since her ten-year-old brother, Ronald, was one of the original group of twenty-two children referred to "The Project."

Three L.A. Unified Schools referred these children because of their learning, behavioral, or leadership issues. I counseled

Ronald on an individual basis over an extended period of time, but I never developed a formal counseling relationship with Annette. However, I did note that Ronald was an observant and insightful child who was very close to and protective of Annette.

Their mother, Christine Caraway, was an original member of the "Core Mothers Group." That group consisted of mothers whose children consistently participated in the project's developing program. I facilitated their weekly group meetings.

As I listened, I learned in great detail much about the realities of their daily lives. This information helped me design and develop relevant community service programs.

THE RESULT: In 2017, "The Watts Project" will be fifty years old and is known in the community as the Kaiser Permanente Watts Counseling and Learning Center.

As a charter member of The Center, Annette has participated in many center programs. I believe Annette was the "family detective" who observed, monitored, and tracked her family's behaviors and dynamics as she sought to understand herself and her family. Within the village of The Center, Annette was a participant-observer who identified with specific personality characteristics of staff members.

For instance, she developed her feisty behavior by identifying with Mrs. M. Thus, she built and enhanced her sense of self. In her book, Annette describes how The Center, as a safe haven and nurturing village, helped her to grow.

BY: *Wilfred D Coggins*, M.S.W.
CENTER FOUNDER 1/31/17

INTRODUCTION

I'm a cosmetologist, a "Hair Doctor," a mother, a grandmother, a sister, a wife, and a mentor with Motivating the Masses Teen Spirit.

I've mentored teenagers for years through Lady Dupree's Hair Salon. I've been a cosmetologist for 37 years. During these years, I found out that I enjoyed mentoring more than styling hair. I found my niche. Speaking to my clients and giving advice filled my days with joy!

Of course, life has not always been this way. I had my share of traumatic experiences. I was traumatized over and over. Before age eight.

In 1965, the Watts Riots broke out. These were the worst riots in US history - lasting five days. So much was lost during this time - including me. That innocent little girl who thought the world was a kind, loving, and a safe place got a rude awakening. There was a devaluing shame of being a black child in 1965. It has taken me 50 years to find my true value. The Center helped me a great deal in my journey. They did the best they could to help me heal.

With the 1992 civil unrest in Los Angeles, the flashbacks and fear returned. My first memory of being snatched by The Walker boys during the 1965 riots came back. It wasn't until writing this book that I discovered a deeper part of me. I was living as though I had it all together, because I believed I did. Outwardly, I dressed to impress - thinking it would make others accept me. The fear, anger, and shame resurfaced.

My flashbacks caused panic attacks. Because I kept busy, I didn't know I was angry. I didn't allow prejudice to waste my time. I also didn't waste my time with people who made destructive decisions. I continued to stay busy in order to not have to deal with the injustices around me.

My environment was toxic. I refused to accept the toxicity as part of my life. I started making up a new reality for my life. I started manifesting what I wanted in life. Since I continued to visualize and manifest a new reality, it became my true reality.

Before my new reality was real, I trusted no one and stayed alone most of the time. The only time I interacted with others was at home, church, or school. I didn't really let others into my space. I never questioned this reality because it was my norm. I had nothing to be ashamed of and nothing

to be angry about. My success came from my stories that I believed.

I wrote this book to share with you my journey toward healing. I hope that as you read through these chapters, you too can find healing within you.

THE CENTER

I had so much rage and so much shame. I didn't know why I felt that way. I always thought I was okay. In reality, I had an immense fear deep inside, and I didn't have the ability to trust anyone. I didn't know how to identify what I felt because of the environment of my village. In the center of my village was the Kaiser Permanente Watts Counseling and Learning Center which was known as "The Center."

When I was a little girl, the Watts Riots traumatized me. Bill Coggins came in a few years later. He is a clinical social worker chosen by Kaiser Permanente to start a program to help the families that were traumatized. When he started The

Center, my family was one of the first families accepted. The reason why we got into the program was because of my brother Ronnie. He did something at school that made them call the social worker. In The Center, we went through group and individual counscling. As a result, it helped me express my feelings. The name of my group at that time was *The Black Sisters*. The reason we chose that name was because of a James Brown song - "Say it loud! I'm black and I'm proud." As we got older, we changed our name to *The Proud Sisters*. The group met once a week. We had other activities to help us get over some of the things that we saw and some of the things that we had been victim to during the riot. Many of us had very low self-esteem.

To be a black child in the 1960s was extremely scary. Being a part of The Center helped me grow into the woman I am today. We went horseback riding, to summer camps, field trips, and Disneyland.

I did things that took my mind off my fear of my Sunday school class exploding. Having someone to talk to was instrumental to my growth. It was helpful to see people from differing demographics at The Center.

It is so important to let people know that you are a resource they can lean into to heal. My focus is on getting others to open their hearts and doors to those who need it. The Center did exactly this for me when I was a child. Thankfully, this great resource, is still available for the people in the community. The resources are still there but they can't do it all. They are there for us, but a lot of the lessons and a lot of the love that I received was from neighbors, The Center members, and others who just opened their hearts and saw me in need and opened their doors. I will be forever grateful.

I return to The Center even today to help me heal from the trauma-drama.

FAMILY

My mother and father both needed AA. My mom and dad normally invited their friends over on the weekends and they'd party. Then, after a while, they would start fighting. When my parents were not drinking, they were hilarious and loving. However, as time passed, the fighting got worse. One day, after my dad went to work, my mom packed all of our belongings and moved. My dad and I were close. Therefore, I felt very angry for years, because I didn't feel that was right - to just disappear while he was at work. I had no idea what was really going on between them at that time. All I knew was that every so often they would break up, and we moved in with somebody. Sometimes, we moved in with nice people, sometimes we didn't. After a few days they'd get back together, get along for a while, and then the whole process would start all over. The last time they separated, my dad died of a heart attack. We tried to move back into our home, but my uncle forged my mom's signature on some paperwork. Our home was taken from us. Again, we didn't have anywhere to go. So, we ended up moving to the projects. It was hard for me to forgive my mother. I felt that my daddy need us, and we abandoned him.

I was very angry with my mom. I felt like if she hadn't left, everything would have been okay. Of course, I didn't know that. It wouldn't haven been. But back then, I thought everything was moms fault. I would go around telling everybody how bad my mom was and how she didn't care about me. She would tell me that I was the reason why he hit her. I didn't believe her. I'm the youngest of six, and they were fighting before I was born. I wasn't the reason. But I couldn't figure out why she would tell me it was my fault.

As the baby of the family, I always had to play catch up. When stuff went on in the family, I knew nothing about it, but all my siblings expected me to know. It was impossible for me to know what was going on when I wasn't there. I asked a lot of questions that they did not want to answer. Even today there are unanswered questions.

For example, I don't understand why my older sister doesn't treat me as her sister. She used to call me "little black ugly girl" so much I thought it was my name. The rest of my siblings accepted me and helped me. My sister Audrey, she had leukemia, she was very loving and caring. She knew what it was like to be treated differently.

Ronnie and I shared the same mother and father. My mother paired us off for safety reasons. Every brother had a sister to protect, and every sister had a brother to be responsible for. Ronnie and I were paired off because of our birth order.

Audrey and Sonny were the same age 6 days annually. Audrey's birthday was the 12th of

December and Sonny's birthday is the 6th of December. That was a problem for my mother because my mother's brother and wife raised Audrey. However, Sonny was raised by my Aunt Roxy (daddy's sister).

When I was born, my oldest sister was sixteen, and my brother Greg was fourteen. By the time I was three years old, they were both out of the house. I didn't get the chance to really get to know them, but I was able to bond with them on other occasions.

My brother, Gregory, was my hero. He went off to be a marine in the Vietnam War. I will never forget the day he came home. He was in uniform, and he had muscles everywhere. I was so happy and proud of him as my brother. I saw him as my protector. I always felt if anybody bothered me, I'd just get my big brother Gregory. That was a false sense of security, but it was my security. It helped me throughout my journey because there was a part of me that was fearless, and then there was a part of me that was totally unequipped to fight. One day the fear overwhelmed me when he got sick and lost a tremendous amount of weight. He had been sprayed with Agent Orange in Vietnam and it was literally killing him. When my protector left, I lost my sense of security.

Over the years, my brother Ronnie, my father, my mother, Audrey, and Gregory all passed away. Sometimes I felt like I had absolutely no family. I had to reach out to others in order to help myself. Family doesn't have to be *blood related*. It can be anyone you make family. You can actually choose the members of your family. And it is so important to choose wisely.

Neighborhood

The people in our neighborhood who knew my mom and dad knew that they fought a lot, and they opened their doors to me. There was a family that lived next door that showed me a lot of love. That's where I hung out and learned how to play baseball, bowl, spades, dominos, and other games. The family environments that I put myself in, the choices that I made, the people that I chose to be around served as my support system.

When I was sixteen years old, my brother Ronnie shot at me. Our neighbor next door was kind enough to let me stay at her house until things got better. She treated me like one of her children. That meant a lot to someone who had nowhere to go.

Then there was my mother's best friend, Sweet Alice. She was another lady who had an influence on me. Remarkably, she had twelve children and always made room and time for me.

I was blessed to be able to attach myself to various families who always welcomed me into their homes.

Some people have been traumatized and just have a hard time feeling as though there is anybody good left in the world. They tend to feel like, "What's the use?" They lose hope. I'm here to share with you, there is always hope. There are people who care about you.

Children, in particular, often do not feel worthy because society doesn't support them. Society shows they don't matter and no one cares. Thankfully, this is the furthest thing from the truth. Society does indeed care. Sometimes you just need to know where to look and from where to receive the support.

ACCIDENT

There was a particular incident when my brother accidentally hit my arm with a palm tree branch. We were at Mrs. Washington's house - our babysitter. Her house was on the same plot of land as ours. Her house was on the front part of the lot while ours was in the back. Mrs. Washington had her own children *and* took care of us. My mom would send us to her when she had to go to work.

Ronnie and I went outside one day to play a game we called "daddy whooper." It involved palm tree branches. Mind you, my mother already warned us to leave those branches alone and not play with them. We didn't listen. Ronnie swung a branch and it hit my arm. One of the needles got stuck in my arm, so we pulled it out.

What we didn't know was that a tiny piece of it was left inside. It went so deep into my arm that it lodged in between two bones. That explained why the doctor couldn't find it when they took X-rays. After what happened that day, my brother and I made a pact to forget about it. We knew our mom would be upset with us.

We didn't tell anyone — not even Mrs. Washington. We told her a different story. She ended up just putting rubbing alcohol and a band-aid on it to help it heal.

School & Surgeries

In the other part of my village was my school. I loved school, but I didn't understand a lot of it. There was a time when I had to miss a lot of school to have four surgeries on my arm – a byproduct of my palm branch accident.

About five or six years after the incident with the palm branches, I was in school when I notice a boil was growing on my arm. Mr. Coggins recommended to my parents to meet with Dr. Ashby to help me heal. Dr. Ashby's office was located on Martin Luther King Boulevard. I will never forget my first visit to his office. Dr. Ashby actually lanced the boil on my arm and let it drain during my first office visit.

That experience was unforgettable because I was awake through the procedure. And so, the office visits and surgeries began.

The various surgeries caused me to be out of school for two to three months at a time. By the time I could attend school again, the lessons were already in sentence structure. Since I missed out on all the basic phonics, I had to catch up to the rest of the class. By the time I figured out how to write a sentence, the boil came back. This made me miss school once again for two to three months - depending on how successful the surgery was. I also had to stay in the hospital for six to seven days, go back home, and then go back to the hospital again to have the dressings changed every week. By the time I got back to school again, my class was learning their multiplication tables. I missed spelling, rules of spelling, writing, and so many vital lessons.

I thought I was dumb because I didn't know what was going on. My test scores landed me in a special class. The school thought I had a learning disability. By the time I got in the special class, I had to go back for yet another surgery.

Back then, they didn't know a lot about cancer. They thought maybe it was some form of cancer. Since the surgeries weren't working, and to stop the cancer from spreading, the decision was made to amputate my arm. The doctors simply couldn't figure out why the infection kept returning.

Mr.Coggins recommended to my parents to try one last thing. He asked them to take me to the Children's Hospital in Los Angeles, California. So, they did.

While I was there, I was initially quite fearful. There was this male nurse who made my fears slowly drift away. I remember this so vividly because I had never seen a male nurse before. This man would come into my room doing the funky chicken. I affectionately named him Mr. Funky Chicken. He would make me laugh. When he gave me a shot, it didn't hurt. I was not afraid of the treatment. There was something about the Children's Hospital that made me feel secure.

I was there for quite some time. At the hospital was where I saw my first pool table ever. We had a recreation room in the hospital where the kids went to watch TV and interact with each other. We played pool and helped one another heal. That was a truly memorable and great experience. I learned the importance of nurses - no matter their gender. Because this was the first male nurse, I felt safe with him.

The needle between the bones was found at the Children's Hospital. Without them, I would have been in the other hospital getting my arm amputated at the elbow. And there would not have been any way that I could have been a cosmetologist. Kaiser Permanente Watts Counseling

and Learning Center saved my
arm.

SANDBOX

Bridgette had a sandbox on her front porch. We played in the sandbox every day. One day we were playing, and Bridgette threw sand at me. So, I threw sand back at her. The sand got *all over* her – from head to toe. It made an absolute mess of her **hair**. Her mother was *furious* with me. She immediately grabbed me by the back of my shirt, dragged me into her house, put me up in a chair over her sink, and told her son to dig a hole in the backyard. I could hear the shovel, I could hear him throwing the dirt, and she put my head over the sink holding a knife. She told me that she would cut my head off and her son was going to bury it and nobody would miss me. Nobody would even care that I was gone.

At that time, when I should have been totally afraid, I was at peace because I had been to church with family and I found out about God. I knew that God loved me and that there was a heaven and that heaven was a better place to be. I stood in the chair, with my head over that sink ready to go, because I thought I was going to a better place. I prayed to God and felt an overwhelming peace. What came over me was so transparent, I think it scared the woman because she immediately stopped, took me out of the chair, and told me to go home. But I never went back to play with Bridgette.

That was quite an experience. I was glad she let me go. But as I got older and as I talked to my counselor about it, the counselor bought something to my attention. She said, "You scared that woman because you were not afraid to die at six years old." How bad do things have to be for a small child to feel that death is a better option than life? That's what scared the woman - so she let me go.

That was the evil part of the village. There's always good and evil. Good and evil doesn't care about your color, or where you live, or your socioeconomic background. Its only concern is good vs. evil. Plain and simple We each have a choice to do good or to do evil. Through continually choosing good, I believe we can make the world a better place for each of us.

THE CHURCH

The church is where I grew spiritually. In my village, our church was one of the well-known churches. People came from miles around for our barbecue. My Uncle Clevester, and my mother taught me about God. He used to tell me, "As long as you are doing what is right, you will never go wrong." And he'd say "Do the Book!" and "Thank God For The Victory Today!" I miss him.

Since Dupree was my first husband's last name, my Auntie always called me Lady Dupree.
At that time, I was working at Mr. T's Hair Clinic, building my clientele. Because I worked at the Hair Clinic, my aunt told me to get a white jacket (like a doctor's

lab coat) and have Lady Dupree put on it. Since I was working at Mr. T's Hair Clinic, she considered me a hair doctor. I believed her. And because of that, my clientele grew tremendously. I started my advertisement with this tagline: Ask for Lady Dupree when you come to Mr. T's Hair Clinic. They did.

BIRTHDAY

On my birthday, I went to the salon and there was a beautiful box perfectly wrapped at my station. My emotions just sky rocketed. I felt so special because somebody actually remembered my birthday. I was so happy. I went to my station and I hurried to open my package. It was a roach motel with a big giant cockroach in it. At that very moment, I knew that I had to get out of there. One of my clients saw the look on my face and the hurt in my eyes. But he didn't say anything.

A few months later, when he came in for his appointment, he gave me a box beautifully wrapped. I was scared to open it, but I did. Inside was a key with a note. The note said, "You can make it on your own." It had an address on it. The address was to my salon.

He told me that I can make it on my own. I was so scared. I was only 23 years old, but I knew my family members were in the hair business also. I called around to see who had equipment I could use. The next thing I knew, I had equipment, supplies, and everything needed for my business. I had my business license. I had a big giant flashing neon sign saying, "Lady Dupree's Hair Salon." It lit up the whole corner of 79th and Figueroa Street.

I thought my gift giver would come and get his hair done at the new salon, but he never did. No one has ever had that much faith in me before.

I told my Uncle Clevester, who was also my pastor, about the salon, and he loaned me a thousand dollars. He told me it was a loan. I assured him that I would give him $50 a week until I paid it in full. He said, "No don't do that. Just put it away and save it for a rainy day. And when you get it all together, then you can pay me - just like I gave it to you, all at one time." And that's exactly what I did.

My grandfather sent me money also. For the first time, I felt like somebody cared for me and that my family was working together. I was so happy. Also, by this time, my mother had stopped drinking. Everything was looking up for my life.

One day I went home and found a friend of mine with my husband. My heart sank. Here I am being blessed on one end and cursed on another – or so it felt. But I didn't give up. My marriage to Mr. Dupree ended that day.
I went to the owner of the building that the salon was in and

asked if I could be the new manager. The person who was managing the 42-unit complex was in his eighties. He was going to retire soon. I knew that as manager, I would get a salary and a apartment. I got the job, and I moved into the apartment close to my Salon.

I didn't have anything. I was broken in so many ways. Yet, it was the end of one thing and the beginning of another. I got to know the seniors that were living in the complex. Little by little, people started giving me things. It was just me and my 2-year-old baby girl.

Healing

My mother and my daughter became my receptionists. My mother went back to the apartment and made sure to meet the school bus make dinner every night. One thing led to another, and she stayed with me for almost eight years. She was a great big help. The same mother that didn't care for me when I was a child, turned out to be the greatest help that I could ever have. The same woman that I talked about how she wasn't ever there for me, helped me get over my ex-husband. She was the one who was there for me when I needed her most.

She was the one who noticed Mr. Bozeman was a good man. Mr.

Bozeman's Aunt Fannie came to California for a visit her and my mother always had him coming by the building to fix something. In no time at all, we were married. My mother and his auntie hooked us up. It's been twenty-nine years and counting.

My family made a complete 180-degree turn. Everything was looking up. But it didn't last long. I started losing each member, one by one.

I got to the point when I was left alone - almost. At one point, it was just me, the sister that didn't claim me, and the long-lost brother that I barely seldom saw - who one time touched me inappropriately. And because he couldn't forgive himself, he didn't come around me.

79TH STREET LIGHT

During this very difficult time, I had The Center to help me once again. The members of the church and the community patronized my business. My *Lady Dupree's* sign was so bright, but I knew what it meant to have such a light. I knew God was telling me to put the sign up there.

I was invited to an event in Palm Springs, CA to celebrate those who have been thirty years sober. One lady got up and said that it was because of a light that blinked on 79th street that her life was spared. You see, this lady, she said that she went to that light, because it was a light in a dark place. When somebody tried to grab her, because she was in that light, she was able to get help. She knew she needed to change her life. That was the testimony that she gave.

She had no idea who I was. She talked about my sign and had no idea that I was even in the room. But hearing that testimony, knowing that it was my light that lit up that corner was the very light that saved her life, has definitely saved mine. After the celebration, I introduced myself to her. She said that a lot of us needed that light.

For a long time, I was afraid to be at this location because I didn't fully understand this gift given to me. I thought the man who gave me the key was someday going to come back and tell me what I owed him. But he never did. I know that he helped me, and I believed that if we try to help others, we can change somebody else's life too.

First Lady Auntie

My uncle grew old. My aunt, who refer to me as Lady Dupree, died. She was the best First Lady. She taught me so much. My uncle, my aunt, and I went on vacation together one year to Canada. I drove their 40-foot mobile home all the way to Canada. My uncle wouldn't stay in a hotel along the way. So, we stayed in the Walmart parking lots.

Making memories is what it was all about. I loved my family. One side of my family was dirt poor while the other was well off. My uncle bought my aunt a Rolls-Royce for her birthday. When we went on outings, she insisted that I drive. We would go shopping. She took time out to show me the "other" side of life. That meant the world to me because what she showed were things I would have otherwise not seen.

The encouragement and hope that she gave me was amazing. I couldn't have ever received it from anyone the way I received it from her. After she died my uncle remarried.

Pastor Uncle

I miss him. I realized he has a new wife and a new family. However, you just don't disregard your old family. But he says he is happy, and that's all that matters.

I reached out to his children. I found out how hard they had to work in their childhood. They always had to sell barbecue every weekend. On Fridays and Saturdays, the lines would be wrapped around the church and they would be there working. I thought they had a good life. I see now that wasn't true.

That trip to Canada gave me an idea on probably why. I'd never worked so much in my life. That was all he knew, work. His children knew Going anywhere with him, meant work. Not a vacation. My uncle was happy when ever he was fishing.

CANCER

When my mom got sick with cancer, I asked her why things were so bad early on. She told me that she was 4 days old when her mother died. Her siblings had to work and the neighborhood kids told her that it was her fault. That she had killed their mother. I asked her, "Was that the reason why you blamed me for my dad's actions?" And she couldn't tell me. She just said, "It's a possibility, because I didn't know how to be a mother, I didn't have one."

Annie Mae Lindsey, her sister in Chicago, helped me understand my mother. When she came to visit us, she taught her how to be a mother. Also, her best friends at the Core Mothers (at The Center) took her under their wings and showed her how to love me. They were the ones who encouraged her to come to my salon and help me. So that's what she did.

Before my mother died, she showed me so much love. I thought I was going to be angry with her for the rest of my life, but she became my very best friend. I was able to forgive her for everything that happened when I was a child. I took care of her the last two years of her life - the way that I wanted her to take care of me when I was a child.

GOD

Remember when I told you that when the lady tried to make me think she was going to kill me, and I wasn't afraid and I didn't cry? I was like, "I believe that God has my back. He was guiding my footsteps. My faith in Him is what allowed me to step out and open my first business. Have you ever question God? In 1992, I questioned God: Why? Why God? It was 1965 all over again. The riots, the burned businesses - I had just moved to a new location - then another riot. I lost everything. I had flashbacks and the fear and anger returned. Mr. Bozeman and I had just bought our first house. We were unpacking boxes when we heard the TV news saying   something like angry people were expressing themselves yet again. This time it took time to get over the pain, fear, and shame.

This time, I was no longer a child. I was years older. That's when I started remembering what really happened in 1965.

Open Your Heart

I really want to share that if we all work together, helping each other, we can accomplish so much more. Because of what Mr. Coggins did, he changed my life. He could have stayed in London and in his private practice. He graduated from UCLA, he earned all the accolades, but he came to us and he wanted to help the less fortunate. He was a light in a dark place – just like my salon. I think that's what happened to me in my salon - I became a light in a dark place.

When I worked on people's hair, I actually helped their lives more than anything else. When the kids came in, I gave them a free hairdo for a good progress report card. I think about all the things people could do for others. For example, look at all of the senior citizens who are living alone and lonely. Now look at all the people who need a place to live. Wouldn't it be something to somehow connect those dots and bring these two groups together. People building people up, not tearing each other down. That's what The Center did for me.

I went through many traumas. If I had not had those resources, I don't think I would have made it. I really don't. I think people need to help people just as The Center did for my family.

Thank you, Lisa, my sister. This is God at work. If you have ever wondered, if you are doing "God's will," allow me to answer: YesYES! You are. Want evidence? I'm determined to find my way back to me - the little girl I lost fifty years ago! Thank you so much, Lisa, my sister in prosperity. My sister in healing. You made me ask myself all the right questions I had never thought to ask.

You've opened my understanding in a way

no one else could. In the "Watts Riots," so much was lost – my innocence. Wow what a BOL (Breakthrough Out Loud!). I gained trauma drama and I now know why I was afraid of people. I remember now. Snatched at five – the final piece of the puzzle #YAYOR (You Are Your Own Rescue).

For more information, contact the author:

ASK LADY DUPREE -- 310 703-7595
LADYDUPREE50@GMAIL.COM &
A.BOZEMAN@SBCGLOBAL.NET